froglets
Learners

Elephants

by Annabelle Lynch

First published in 2014 by
Franklin Watts
338 Euston Road
London NW1 3BH

Franklin Watts Australia
Level 17/207 Kent Street
Sydney NSW 2000

Picture credits: Galyna Andrushko/Shutterstock: 8.
Brytta/istockphoto: 12. Rich Carey/Shutterstock: 5.
Four Oaks/Shutterstock: 1, 9, 16 Anton Ivanov/
Shutterstock: front cover. Jonathan Pledger/
Shutterstock: 21. Villiers Steyn/Shutterstock: 15.
Johan Swanepoel/Shutterstock: 6-7. Mari Swanepoel/
Shutterstock: 10. Tristan Tan/Shutterstock: 4.
Peter G. De Witt/Dreamstime: 19.

Every attempt has been made to clear copyright.
Should there be any inadvertent omission please
apply to the publisher for rectification.

A CIP catalogue record for this book is
available from the British Library.

Dewey number: 428.6

ISBN 978 1 4451 2910 5 (hbk)
ISBN 978 1 4451 3045 3 (pbk)
Library eBook ISBN 978 1 4451 2916 7

Series Editor: Julia Bird
Picture Researcher: Diana Morris
Series Advisor: Catherine Glavina
Series Designer: Peter Scoulding

Printed in China

Franklin Watts is a division of Hachette Children's Books,
an Hachette UK company. www.hachette.co.uk

Contents

What are elephants? 4

Elephant families 6

Baby elephants 8

Trunks 10

Tusks 12

Eating and drinking 14

Keeping cool 16

Elephant talk 18

Protecting elephants 20

Glossary 22

Quiz 23

Answers and Index 24

The words in **bold** can be found in the glossary.

What are elephants?

Elephants are the biggest **mammals** that live on land. They are found in Africa and Asia.

Asian elephant

African elephants are bigger and heavier than Asian elephants.

African elephant

Elephant families

Elephants are friendly. They live in groups called herds. There are around 10 to 20 elephants in a herd.

The oldest female elephant usually leads the herd.

Baby elephants

Elephant mothers take good care of their babies. Babies stay close to their mother and feed from her milk for two years or more.

Elephant babies are called calves.

Trunks

All elephants have
a long, bendy trunk.
They use it to breathe,
smell and touch things.
It also helps them to
eat and drink.

If an elephant rolls up its trunk and
tucks it under its chin, look out!
It may be about to run at you.

Tusks

Most elephants have two long front teeth called tusks. They use them to dig for food and water, and to **defend** themselves. Tusks are made of **ivory**.

Elephants usually use one tusk more than the other.

Eating and drinking

Elephants eat and drink all day long. They love to eat plants such as grass, leaves, fruit and even flowers.

To drink, elephants suck water up with their trunk and spray it into their mouth.

keeping cool

Elephants live in hot places so they need to keep cool. They splash in water or cover their skin in thick, cool mud.

Flapping their ears helps elephants to keep cool.

Elephant talk

Elephants **trumpet** loudly with their trunks and make deep, **rumbling** sounds. This helps them to keep in touch and stay together as a herd.

Elephants often say hello by touching trunks.

Protecting elephants

We must look after elephants. They are **hunted** for their tusks. The wild places where they live are also disappearing.

There are around 450,000–700,000 African elephants and only 35,000–40,000 Asian elephants living in the wild today.

Glossary

defend – to protect from danger

hunt – to track down an animal and kill it

ivory – a type of bone

mammal – animals with hair that give birth to babies instead of laying eggs. They feed their babies with milk

rumbling – a low noise that goes on and on

trumpet – a loud noise made by blowing out of an elephant's trunk

Websites:

http://kids.nationalgeographic.com/kids/

animals/creaturefeature/african-elephant/

http://kids.sandiegozoo.org/animals/mammals/afri-

can-elephant

Quiz

1. Which elephants are bigger – African or Asian elephants?

2. What are elephant groups called?

3. What are elephant babies called?

4. Name two things that elephants use their trunks for.

5. Why do elephants cover their skin in mud?

6. Why do people hunt elephants?

Answers

1. African elephants
2. Herds
3. Calves
4. Breathe, smell, touch things, eat or drink
5. To keep cool
6. For their tusks

Index

African elephants 4–5, 21   herds 6–7, 18
Asian elephants 4–5, 21

                                     keeping cool 16–17
baby elephants 8–9   keeping in touch 18–19

food and drink 14–15   trunks 10–11, 14, 18
                                     tusks 12–13, 20